CASTLES

Brian Milton

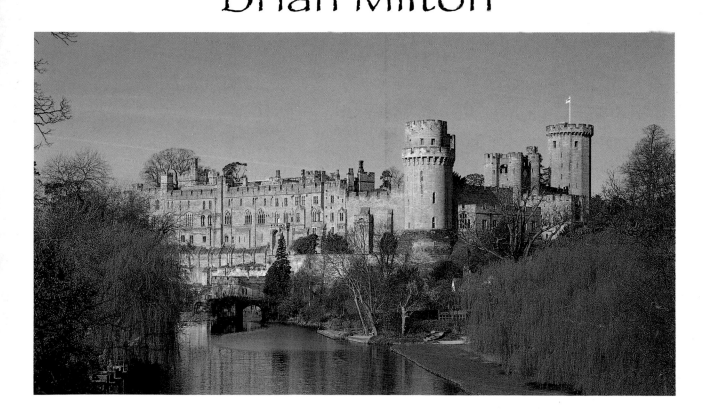

W

FRANKLIN WATTS

© Franklin Watts 1993
This edition: 2002

Franklin Watts
96 Leonard Street
London EC2A 4XD

Franklin Watts Australia
56 O'Riordan Street
Alexandria, Sydney, NSW 2015

ISBN: 0 7496 4573 3 (pbk)

Dewey Decimal Classification: 728.8

A CIP catalogue record for this book is
available from the British Library

Editor: Sarah Ridley
Designer: Janet Watson
Photographer: Martyn Chillmaid
Consultant: Brian Davison
Picture researcher: Joanne King

Acknowledgements: the publishers wish to
thank the staff and children of Merridale
Primary School, Wolverhampton and Corrina
Jacob of Warwick Castle.

Additional photographs: Bridgeman Art Library
11t, 11b; BTA/ETB/Syndication International
7b; Collections 7c, 13tr, 13tl, 13bl, 23cr, 23bl;
e t archive 21c; Chris Fairclough 30; Robert
Harding Picture Library/British Museum 11c;
M Holford 6tr, 7t, 15br; Royal Armouries 23tr,
23tl, 31bl; Warwick Castle contents br, 20r, 21b,
29t; David Williams Photo Library 13br.

Artwork: pg 10 Ed Dovey.

Printed in Malaysia

Contents

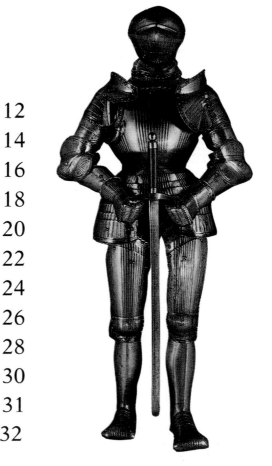

What are castles?

Castles are the protected homes of lords or kings. They were built to provide defence against enemies as well as to make a base from which to impose the authority of the lord on the surrounding area. They also needed to be a comfortable place to live. Most castles in Britain were built between 1066 and 1485.

Castles were the headquarters for the lord's estate. In peace, a small number of soldiers were housed there. In war, the castle provided shelter for the lord's relatives, dependents and a larger number of soldiers.

The building of a castle at Warwick was ordered by William I in 1068. By 1260, the original wooden structure had been replaced by one made of stone. Many changes and extensions took place between 1260 and 1445. The main rooms we see today were refurbished in the 18th century when the castle became a stately home. The exterior has changed little since that time.

What do you think of when you hear the word 'castle'? Have you visited any castles in Britain or abroad? Draw a picture of your own imaginary castle.

5

Why and when were castles built?

The king rewarded his most loyal followers with a grant of land. Castles were built to defend and impose authority over this land. To help pay for the castle and its upkeep, the lord was allowed to collect taxes from those living around the castle. In exchange, the lord and his castle gave protection to the tax-payers in times of war.

Castles were built in England from 1066 onwards. In Wales, the Normans built castles during the 11th, 12th and early 13th centuries but castle-building reached its peak of achievement during the reign of Edward I (1272-1307).

Rochester Castle was built by William I in the south-east of England to help defend his conquest of that area. It is mentioned in the Domesday Book of 1088. The keep dates from 1127.

Find out all you can about castles from the books in the library.

LET'S INVESTIGATE

Over 2000 castles were built in Great Britain between 1066 and 1485 so there should be a castle or a castle site somewhere near you. It may be a large one, like Warwick Castle, or a small ruin. Whichever it is, find out about it as it is part of your local history.

Dover Castle was built during the reign of Henry II (1154-1189) and extended by King John (1199-1216). It is situated on a cliff overlooking the sea to France. This is a good defensive position to warn off any attackers.

Conwy Castle was built between 1283 and 1287. It is one of the most important castles built in Wales by Edward I (1272-1307) to control the Welsh people. It was hated by the Welsh because it was very difficult to attack and represented the replacement of the Welsh princes by English kings.

Craigmillar Castle is only 3 miles from Edinburgh and was begun in the late 14th century. Keeps like this continued to be built in Scotland long after they were stopped in England.

Where were castles built?

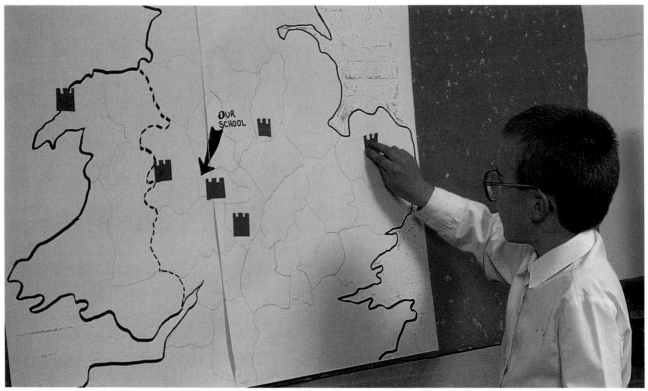

When the Normans invaded Britain, they found a rich country that was already densely populated with villages and towns. The main idea behind their castles was to secure the land around them as quickly as possible. So, the site selected for a new castle was often chosen to be near the established settlements, as well as the roads and rivers that connected them.

When new lands were conquered, castles were also built along the borders of that land to protect it and to establish power over the newly-won territory. Where the natural features of the land could be used to add to the

Using information books and maps, find out where your nearest castles are situated and whether they are built by the sea, on a river or on a hill.

defence of the castle, this was done. So castles are often built beside the sea, or on rivers, hills and rocky outcrops. Choosing the right site on which to build a castle was very important.

Later on, when a lord wanted to build a castle on land given by the king, he had to make application to the king for a 'licence to crenellate'. By this method the king strictly controlled castle building as well as maintaining power over his followers.

Many castles are built on high ground. This makes a castle difficult to attack. It also looks very impressive and can dominate a town and give a commanding view of the surrounding land. If no natural high ground was available, castle builders often created their own mounds. Many early castles were wooden buildings on top of earth mounds encased in timber to make them more difficult to attack.

Water can offer castles some natural protection making it difficult to attack from the sea or across a river or lake. Many stone-built castles had a moat, a ditch designed to be flooded with water. Even moats that were only centimetres deep could prevent attackers from digging their way under the walls of the castle, as their tunnels would constantly flood.

Some castles marked the edge of a king's territory and were used to defend that area from attack. Edward I built castles along the borders of Wales. Another area is the border land between Scotland and England. Some castles were linked with towns over which they stand guard.

Who built and lived in castles?

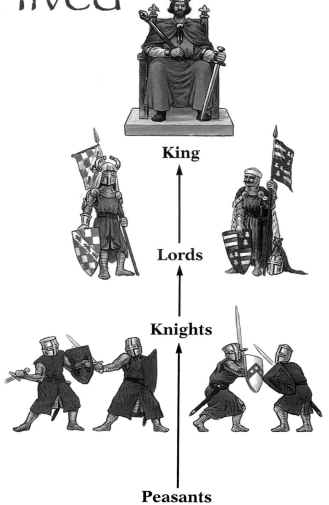

King

Lords

Knights

Peasants

During the main castle building period in this country the king, who needed to raise armies to fight his battles, made payments of land to his lords in exchange for a promise of knights and other fighting men to help with his wars. Lords also granted land to knights and religious leaders in exchange for soldiers. Many merchants and craftsmen served the needs of the rich people.

Peasants came at the bottom of this social order, known as feudalism. They worked the land for the lords and knights, keeping only a percentage of their crops for themselves.

LET'S INVESTIGATE

Fighting was rare so most castle life revolved around hunting, dancing and a variety of games and activities. Find out what people of the period enjoyed doing in their spare time. This will vary depending on their place in the feudal system.

Kings, lords and knights either owned or lived in castles. Many peasants worked the land surrounding castles so the castle was the centre of most people's lives in the Middle Ages.

Dancing was enjoyed by everybody. The knights and their ladies danced as couples to show their courtly love. Peasant dances involved lines or circles of people, often singing and holding hands. Special dances were used as entertainment.

Jousting was a friendly contest between two mounted knights. They tried to unsaddle each other with a blow of the lance. The competition had strict rules and was a popular event at weddings or on other special occasions.

The poor ate simply, mainly bread with small quantities of meat, cheese, milk and butter. The rich feasted well on large amounts of meat and fish, including delicacies such as swan and partridge.

Building materials

As you approach a castle for the first time, take a look at what it is made of. What type of stone is used and how big are the blocks?

Many of the earliest castles were wooden-framed. They took about a year to build but could be burnt down easily. Stone castles presented many construction problems, including quarrying the stone, transporting the stone to the site, organising the workforce and supplying other materials, such as wood and lead. However, when built, the stone castle was a very powerful building which was easily defended and difficult to destroy.

Warwick Castle was constructed of a local sandstone. Heavy materials were probably transported to the castle by river as it was easier to move heavy objects by water than by land. The first castle on the site was built of wood. It was converted to stone between 1070 and 1260 and later enlarged.

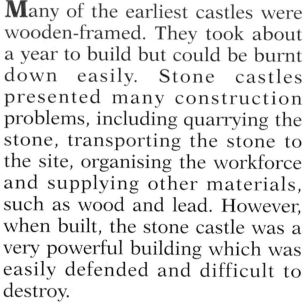

When you visit a castle, compare the size of the stone used to build the castle walls with modern bricks. One stone at Warwick was nearly 2 metres long by half a metre wide.

Sandstone consists of compacted grains of sand. Its colour varies from place to place. The sandstone at Warwick is very strong and has lasted a long time.

In parts of south-east England and East Anglia, castles were built of flints. Flints are nodules of hard stone found in chalk. Lewes Castle was built using this method.

▼ In some areas of the country, sandstone is reddish in colour rather than yellow. It is a hard, well-wearing rock. Bothwell Castle is built of red sandstone.

▲ Limestone is a common rock found in many parts of the country. There are different types of limestone but some make excellent building material. Rockingham Castle is an example of a castle built from limestone.

Some castles were built from local rubble and then 'faced' with stone from other places. Porchester Castle is 'faced' with stone from Caen in Normandy.

13

The motte and bailey

Many early castles centred on a mound of earth (motte), surrounded by a ditch. A tower was erected on top of the mound to act as a refuge in time of war or as the living quarters for the lord and his family. At the foot of the mound was an enclosure known as the bailey, surrounded by a ditch and a wooden wall (palisade).

William the Conqueror and his followers built motte and bailey castles as they conquered England. Having landed in September 1066, William had built his first castle by the time of the Battle of Hastings a month later. However, this would have been a very basic structure. A proper motte and bailey castle took at least a year to build.

The motte at Warwick Castle was constructed on a stone outcrop in 1068 to control the Saxon town of Warwick.

The bailey would have housed all the important rooms; the Great Hall, formal reception room, chapel, kitchen, guest rooms, stables and workshops for wheelwrights, blacksmiths and armourers.

You could make your own castle using paper, cardboard, paper mache, glue and paints. This castle started as a motte and bailey castle and then other parts were gradually added on, as happened with many castles.

On top of the motte, these children have built a tower. Originally it would have been made of wood, but theirs is a stone tower. Their palisade has become a stone wall and there are towers and a well-fortified gate area around the bailey.

The great tower, sometimes called a 'keep' or 'donjon', was a feature of Norman castles. It was built as a residence and as a last line of defence.

The castle defences

One of the main reasons for building castles was to be safe from attack. Walls surround castles and are often strengthened by towers. This gives the name curtain walls, meaning 'walls hung up between towers'. Some castles were built with two sets of curtain walls, one behind the other. Having breached one wall, attackers would be faced with another wall to break down.

Wall-walks meant that defenders could move quickly from one position to another as attackers changed their point of attack.

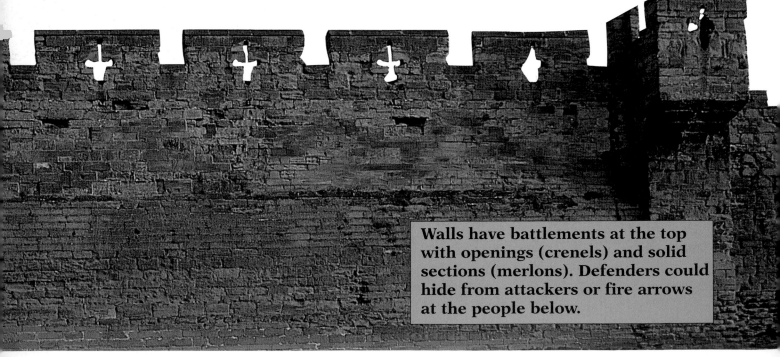

Walls have battlements at the top with openings (crenels) and solid sections (merlons). Defenders could hide from attackers or fire arrows at the people below.

As well as its protecting walls, Warwick Castle gained additional defence through its site close to the River Avon.

The ditch at Warwick Castle helped to defend it by slowing down an enemy's attack and making it difficult to move battering rams close to the walls.

Towers were placed at intervals around the walls. They were higher than the walls and jutted out from them. This allowed defenders to aim missiles at those attacking the base of the walls.

The gatehouse and other defences

The weakest point in the defence of a castle was the gatehouse. This was the only way to enter or leave. Therefore it needed to be the most heavily defended area.

As castles developed, the methods of defence became more elaborate. Some castles were

The bridge at Warwick Castle is the site of the old drawbridge.

The main door to the castle, which was made of wood, would be protected by a portcullis which could be lowered.

almost impregnable until the invention of cannons which could blast holes in doors and walls.

The last time in England that castles were defended was during the Civil War (1643-6). During the war, castles captured by the Parliamentarians, who were fighting the king, were 'slighted'. This meant that sections of the walls and towers were blown up making the castle no use as a fortress. Many castles fell into disrepair after this period.

In most castles slits can be seen in the walls at regular intervals. Archers could stand behind these and aim arrows through the slits. These slits vary in design from straight lines to different types of crosses.

A sally door through which defenders could 'sally' or burst out to make raids on the enemy.

Murder holes were set above the door and the portcullis and could be used for dropping things on attackers or for pouring water on doors which had been set alight.

Machicolations, stone platforms with holes, allowed defenders to safely drop objects on attackers. Originally they were made of wood and were easy to destroy.

Arms and armour

Battles were fought between armies at close quarters and involved a great deal of hand-to-hand fighting. Therefore the knight needed a lot of body protection. This was provided by his shield, body armour and armour for his horse.

Body protection for fighters goes back a long way. 5,000 years ago leather was used, then chain mail and finally metal armour. In the Middle Ages every part of the body was covered in metal. When bullets were developed, armour became of little use.

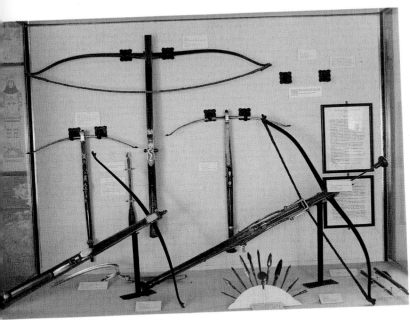

The bolts fired from crossbows were forceful and caused great damage. William Tell, a hero of Switzerland, used a crossbow to shoot at an apple on his son's head at 80 paces.

Plate armour began in the 13th century when soldiers wore a metal breast plate and leg cover (greave). By the 14th century, full plate armour was worn.

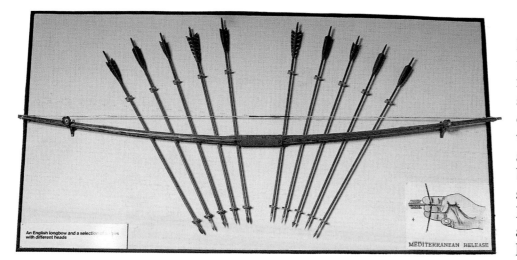

An English longbow and a selection of arrows with different heads

MEDITERRANEAN RELEASE

English armies used longbows made from wood such as elm, yew or birch. They were accurate and arrows could be fired in rapid succession. Robin Hood was a great English longbowman.

In 1346, at the Battle of Crechy, the longbowmen of the English army defeated the mounted knights and crossbowmen of the French army. This was the first time that a mounted army of noble knights had been defeated by ordinary footsoldiers.

Swords were the knights' main weapon. This large black sword belonged to Guy of Warwick.

It is a rare example of an early 14th century double-handed sword. It is 1.66 metres long and weighs 6.8 kilograms.

Field armour was light and flexible for fighting purposes. Jousting armour was much heavier to make the contest safer.

21

Prisoners and punishment

A dungeon was an area of the castle where prisoners were kept. Dungeons were often below ground and were usually dark, airless places. Inside some dungeons was another area called an oubliette. This was a dark space, sometimes under the floor, where there was just room to lie. The word oubliette comes from the French verb *oublier* which means 'to forget'.

The dungeon at Warwick is below ground. It was used for unimportant prisoners awaiting judgement. Knights and lords, usually held prisoner for ransom purposes, were kept in comfortable rooms in the tower.

"This dark, damp, cold, smelly place. Bread and water once a day. A trap forever. No light to see, in a search for food," wrote one child after visiting Warwick Castle's dungeon.

? LET'S INVESTIGATE

Imagine you are a prisoner held at Warwick Castle. Write a diary of your thoughts. A lot of prisoners were kept in castle dungeons during the Civil War (1643-6). Find out more about this period of history.

Torture is a method of inflicting pain on someone to make them confess to a crime or provide information they are not willing to give. Many terrible methods of torture were devised in the Middle Ages.

Shackles were placed around the ankles and then a chain was attached to a wall. This meant that movement was very restricted.

Thumbscrews were metal rings placed around the thumbs and gradually tightened. Eventually the thumbs would be crushed.

Sometimes people were publicly punished by being put in the stocks. Their head and arms were placed through a wooden frame which was then locked. Passersby would throw food at them.

People were stretched on the rack until their limbs were torn from their sockets.

Drawbridge and portcullis models

Whole rooms in gatehouse towers were given over to the machines that operated the drawbridge and portcullises. A portcullis is a gate that slides up and down. If the enemy tried to rush in to the castle, it was much quicker and more effective to drop a portcullis down rather than force heavy doors closed against the incoming force. Investigate how drawbridges and portcullises work.

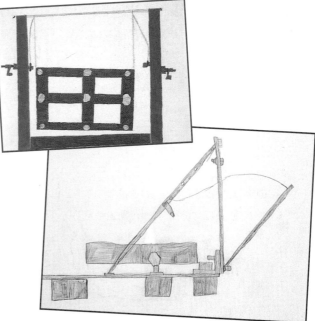

Making sketches of your drawbridge or portcullis is a good start.

Using your sketches, try out some design ideas.

The mechanisms in the drawings and models are very simple and could be made with a minimum of equipment. You could design much more complicated methods for raising and lowering your models.

Think about the following points:

- How can the model be easily raised?
- How can it be made to stay up?
- Can it be easily lowered?

You could make models from any type of construction material. You will probably need some strong string. Not much else is needed except a lot of discussion and a great deal of experimenting.

When you have built your model, check that it works.

These models were made by children. Can you see ways to improve them?

Sieges and siege machines

Castles were so well defended that it could take time to wear them down. A prolonged attack was called a siege. Sometimes the only way to get inside was to wait for the occupants' food and water to run out. This was called a blockade. It could take some time. The blockade of Kenilworth Castle in 1266 lasted 6 months.

Attackers used siege machines to weaken the defences. These machines fired objects, rammed walls and doors, or helped the attackers over the walls. Another way to penetrate defences was by tunnelling under the castle walls.

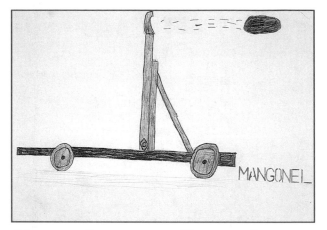

Mangonels were small catapults, designed to throw a stone the size of a football about 150 metres. Draw your own mangonel.

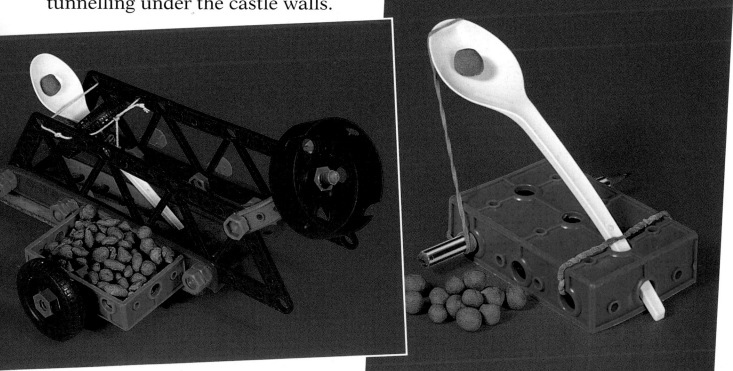

Design your own mangonel, using basic materials. The difficult part is getting enough tension on the weapon-holder so that, when released, the object shoots forward.

Test your mangonel by seeing how far it can throw objects. As well as distance, remember that objects were fired over walls.

Another type of siege machine was the belfry, a movable tower as high, or higher, than the castle walls. This could be rolled up to the wall and a drawbridge on the top level lowered so that the attackers could fight hand-to-hand with the defenders. Ladders to each floor meant that other men could replace those on the top floor, if necessary.

Humpty Dumpty was a siege tower used in the Civil War. Research siege towers and draw your own.

27

Shields and banners

Shields were made in a variety of shapes. The shape featured on these pages is the Norman shield most popular during the Crusades (1096-1270) when armies from Christian Europe fought the Islamic armies of the Turks and Arabs.

When knights were engaged in tournaments or battles they were clothed in armour. It was obviously important to know who was under the armour, so emblems were worn on the shield and the sur-coat, which gives us the name coat-of-arms. When a knight married a wealthy knight's daughter, both coats-of-arms were shown. Over time, the coat-of-arms could be used to represent all the important descendants.

Try designing your own coat-of-arms. It is important to think about what information you want to display.

What does this shield tell you about the school for which it was designed?

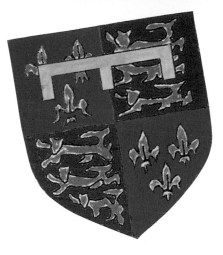

Shields were used to protect the side of the body that was not holding a weapon. In use from the earliest times, they are still used today by police to control riots.

Flags were important for battle and for hoisting above a castle. They were made out of a piece of cloth with a design on them and again could be used to identify people in battle. Lords had a rectangular flag, called a gonfalon. Knights carried a pennon which was smaller than the gonfalon and forked at the outer edge. An esquire carried a small triangular flag called a pennoncel or pencil.

These are some of the banners of the Earls of Warwick which are now hanging in the castle armoury.

29

Model of a castle

The picture shows a model of a castle with curtain walls, towers, gatehouse and a keep. With the help of the picture, together with the information in the book, you could build a model castle.

Points to think about

1) Collect the materials you will need. Don't forget things like adhesive, scissors or paint.
2) Prepare the place where you will build the model.
3) Make basic designs and drawings and develop these to help with your model building.
4) Build your model giving consideration to the suitability of various materials and your ability to handle equipment.
5) If you come up against problems, try to find alternative methods.
6) Think about how successful you have been and share your ideas with other people.

Glossary

Arrow-loop or slit
The vertical opening in the walls through which arrows were shot.

Bailey
The courtyard inside the castle walls.

Battlements The top part of a tower or wall.

Crenel
The name for the gaps in the battlements through which arrows could be fired.

Curtain
The general name for the walling of a castle.

Donjon
Another name for the **Great tower**.

Dungeon
The modern word for the area of the castle used to keep prisoners.

Drawbridge
The wooden bridge which could be raised or lowered.

Great tower
The main tower of the castle.

Keep
Another name for the **Great tower**.

Machicolation
Projecting part of the battlements with holes in the floor.

Mangonel
A stone-throwing machine.

Merlon
The higher solid part of the battlements between the crenel gaps. Soldiers sheltered behind this solid stone when under attack.

Motte
A mound of earth.

Murder-holes
Openings in the roof above main gate.

Oubliette
Small dungeon area.

Portcullis
Grill gate used to protect main gate.

Sally port
Small postern door in the tower.

Index